Love Light Healing's
Daily Self-Love
Messages

REBECCA SLAVEN

BALBOA.
PRESS

A DIVISION OF HAY HOUSE

Balboa Press books may be ordered through booksellers or by contacting:

Balboa Press
A Division of Hay House
1663 Liberty Drive
Bloomington, IN 47403
www.balboapress.com
1 (877) 407-4847

Because of the dynamic nature of the Internet, any web addresses or links contained in this book may have changed since publication and may no longer be valid. The views expressed in this work are solely those of the author and do not necessarily reflect the views of the publisher, and the publisher hereby disclaims any responsibility for them.

The author of this book does not dispense medical advice or prescribe the use of any technique as a form of treatment for physical, emotional, or medical problems without the advice of a physician, either directly or indirectly. The intent of the author is only to offer information of a general nature to help you in your quest for emotional and spiritual well-being. In the event you use any of the information in this book for yourself, which is your constitutional right, the author and the publisher assume no responsibility for your actions.

Any people depicted in stock imagery provided by Getty Images are models, and such images are being used for illustrative purposes only. Certain stock imagery © Getty Images.

Print information available on the last page.

ISBN: 978-1-9822-0181-4 (sc)
ISBN: 978-1-9822-0183-8 (hc)
ISBN: 978-1-9822-0182-1 (e)

Library of Congress Control Number: 2018904259

Balboa Press rev. date: 08/16/2018

Welcome to the Year of Self-Love

Love Light Healing's

Daily Self-Love Messages

By: Rebecca Slaven

This book is dedicated to my sons,
Aidan and Willie.

January

January 1

Today's Self-Love Message:

From this moment forward, always love and accept yourself for all that you are.

This is your life to love.

January 2

Today's Self-Love Message:

You are worth every effort and are a valuable asset in the world. Always know how much the people in your life love you. Value and love yourself so that you can do the same for others.

Share love with those around you.

January 3

Today's Self-Love Message:

Awaken to your experience and celebrate who you are. Each day is a new opportunity to manifest your heart's desire.

Have immense gratitude for yourself.

January 4

Today's Self-Love Message:

When you need help, ask for it!
When you need a friend, reach out to those who love you. Know that you always have a support team.

You are surrounded by love.

January 5

Today's Self-Love Message:

Engage with yourself. Take a walk in the woods or even just around the house. With each step, repeat to yourself that you love and accept all that you are.

You are at home in your heart.

January 6

Today's Self-Love Message:

Be patient with yourself- you are enough!

Allow the experience.

January 7

Today's Self-Love Message:

I am happy, healthy, and loved!

Repeat this phrase often to create more happiness, love, and health in your life.

Words are powerful.

January 8

Today's Self-Love Message:

Create time to rest. At least once a month, let relaxation be the only agenda. What makes you feel at ease? Can you make more space for that in your life starting today?

Let it be easy and rest.

January 9

Today's Self-Love Message:

All you can be is the best version of your present moment self. Let your mind be filled with positive thoughts about the person you are. Live your happiest life!

Focus on what brings you joy.

January 10

Today's Self-Love Message:

It is important to acknowledge good days. Sometimes it just flows. Appreciate these moments.

Live your life.

January 11

Today's Self-Love Message:

You must first love all the parts of yourself. You are the most unique creation of art. You have the ability to love and the right to be happy. Embrace all that you are! The things that you have imagined are your shortcomings will one day be the reason for something great.

Believe in yourself.

January 12

Today's Self-Love Message:

Hold on to hope and appreciate the moment. What does holding onto hope look like? It means instead of letting a bump in the road take you down, remember that it is a passing phase. The more you can create a positive response despite the outcome, the easier you will be able to return to a state of contentment.

Be your own peace.

January 13

Today's Self-Love Message:

Never give up on yourself. Trusting yourself is the only way through every situation in life.

You are capable!

January 14

Today's Self-Love Message:

It's important to have people in your life who you care about because it is a reminder of how much you are loved. Think about how it feels when you see someone you really love; it's wonderful, right? Well, that someone loves you just as much! That's such a great part of being alive- to love and be loved.

You are loved.

January 15

Today's Self-Love Message:

Be kindest to the parts of yourself that you are working on. Love yourself through every change. Be good to the person you are right now. This is how progress is made.

Each part of your life is important.

January 16

Today's Self-Love Message:

There will be days when living in your own skin will feel like too much. It is in these moments that your consciousness is asking you to shed and begin anew.

What can you let go of today?

January 17

Today's Self-Love Message:

Listen to your intuition. Be willing to put as much faith in yourself as you do in external forces. Believe in your own guidance system.

Support your dreams.

January 18

Today's Self-Love Message:

Consider the number of people who think of you daily with such warmth and kindness. Always remember how much you are loved. It is the most amazing feeling when you let that really sink in.

Be LOVED!

January 19

Today's Self-Love Message:

Each of you is a gift to the world. Notice how even the tiniest stars still light up the sky and recognize how meaningful each one is. What will your legacy be?

What do you really want? Go get it!

January 20

Today's Self-Love Message:

Never give up! Always believe that your goals, passions, and hopes are possible. Love is stronger than any fear you may have. Have faith that your love will carry you through. Believe in the power that lives inside of you.

Let love be your guiding force.

January 21

Today's Self-Love Message:

Be brave and go after what your heart desires. If you fall, learn how to pick yourself up again. Love your bruises. The relationship you have with yourself is so important. You only get stronger the more often you pursue what makes you happy.

Care for yourself with loving-kindness.

January 22

Today's Self-Love Message:

Take it one day at a time; it makes it all seem a little less overwhelming. Try it this week. Just plan one day really well and don't worry about what has happened before or what is coming next.

Be present for each of your best days.

January 23

Today's Self-Love Message:

Let go of needing to be validated and instead choose to be good enough right now. Give yourself compliments from the person who knows you better than anyone - YOU.

You are worthy of your happiest life.

January 24

Today's Self-Love Message:

One way to love yourself is to find out what makes you happy and gives you strength. Whatever it is that ignites the spark, nurture it with all that you have. When you shine your light, many people will attempt to blow it out through unwarranted criticism, judgment, and false words - good, let them. When these things happen, rather than say they stole the light/show/love/happiness, thank them because when you have built a strong fire, blowing air only makes it grow brighter.

Now watch your light grow.

January 25

Today's Self-Love Message:

When you feel happy, it shows in everything. Next time you feel immensely happy, take a picture of your smile. Look at it when you need a reminder of what lifts you up.

SMILE BIG - LOVE MORE

January 26

Today's Self-Love Message:

Laughing is a way in which you can bring happiness back to the front of your subconscious. When you smile, you raise your frequency and lighten your mood. Create more moments in your life to be joyful about.

Laughter is a sure way to change your mind.

January 27

Today's Self-Love Message:

Loving yourself means accepting who you are when others may not respond well to even your best intentions. The only way to do such a great task is to still love yourself when the world presents you with reasons to think otherwise. Keep being loyal to yourself and have unshakeable confidence in the person you are.

The love you have for yourself will surpass even the hardest of days.

January 28

Today's Self-Love Message:

Be good to yourself no matter what! The only person who really understands you is you. Be thankful for your own contributions to this life. It is amazing what you can bring to the world when you shine your own light.

You are spectacular.

January 29

Today's Self-Love Message:

Life pushes your boundaries. This happens so you will know how capable you are of handling whatever comes your way.

Experience everything.

January 30

Today's Self-Love Message:

There are so many ways to find happiness from within. These tried and true methods have worked:
- Meditate every day even if it's for 5 minutes
- Smile often
- Give something away
- Move your body

Today, and every day, accept all that you are.

January 31

Today's Self-Love Message:

The choice of what you focus on at any given moment is always yours. In most cases, your days are filled with more good than bad, but you can be so consumed with negativity that you miss it. If you moved your focus to honoring all the brightness that surrounds you each day, the darkness would cease to exist.

Be thankful for the good things in life.

February

February 1

Today's Self-Love Message:

Sometimes self-love means walking away from what no longer makes you happy. Have the courage to take the first step. Then every day, keep walking in the new direction. Pave your path and make it your own!

It is worth the risk to listen to your heart.

February 2

Today's Self-Love Message:

The list of things to do is never done. Instead of letting it get to you, be excited about everything that you have. Sometimes you must allow yourself the chance to rest and escape. You can take a break knowing that next week, and every single one thereafter, you will still have laundry to fold.

Take it easy.

February 3

Today's Self-Love Message:

Know you are always worthy of your greatest potential. Everything you desire wants to have you. All it takes is to imagine what is possible. Once you realize your dream, send it out to the universe and be ready to receive.

You are the greatest potential!

February 4

Today's Self-Love Message:

Hold on to the dream that one day you will be where you want to be. As you travel on your journey, appreciate the moments when everything feels right in the world. By acknowledging these positive times, you bring more of them into your life.

Everything you want is coming to you now.

February 5

Today's Self-Love Message:

Believe in the greatest version of yourself. It is a true picture of what your life can be. Practice the law of attraction by believing that you are receiving everything you need to manifest your dreams. You are the greatest version of yourself right now! It will only get better from here.

Believe in your capability to succeed!

February 6

Today's Self-Love Message:

If all the negativity you encountered was compared to all the positivity in your life, it is guaranteed the positive influences would be much greater. The reason you remember the bad times more is because of the good that it stole from you. Next time something terrible happens, acknowledge it, and then immediately go do something to match that darkness with a positive expansive light.

Keep bringing your mind back to what works!

February 7

Today's Self-Love Message:

Loving yourself doesn't come with specific instructions on how to fix what has been broken. Instead, it comes with an opportunity to be just as you are and to love yourself through it all.

Arrive exactly as you are.

February 8

Today's Self-Love Message:

Follow your heart. Ask yourself what you need and really listen. It's worth it!

Love the entirety of your being.

February 9

Today's Self-Love Message:

Trust your instinct and follow your gut. Sometimes you feel nervous because it is going to be the best thing that ever happened, and your body senses that. Pay attention to what you feel in different experiences so that you can recognize how connected you are to everything happening around you.

Be in tune with your intuition.

February 10

Today's Self-Love Message:

Many people seek approval from the outside world. It is natural to want others to appreciate and value you as a person. One of the best things you can do is give others your stamp of approval! Can you imagine if everyone did that?

Approve of yourself and others.

February 11

Today's Self-Love Message:

Nourish your own soul by curling up, staying home, and caring only about what you want in this moment. It is possible to relax and be happy with more to do another day.

There is always tomorrow.

February 12

Today's Self-Love Message:

Wake up in peace knowing you have given yourself the space to rest. Allow for the feelings of a fresh start to rush over you. Make it count and embrace each precious moment!

Cultivate a life you are excited to wake up to.

February 13

Today's Self-Love Message:

How do you overcome your negative self-talk? Check in with yourself regularly and ask if this is what you want to be creating. Write out whatever you are feeling and let it all pour onto the pages. Afterwards, re-read the passage and summarize it using the power of positivity. Change your bad days into proud moments because you overcame them!

Be bright!

February 14

Today's Self-Love Message:

Whether today is spent with someone you love or by yourself, be kind to every person you encounter. Use today as a tool to share as much as you can with yourself and those who you love. Love without holding back.

Celebrate love.

February 15

Today's Self-Love Message:

Believe that your own self-worth is more important than ever before. Turn inward and observe how far you have come. Set up reminders to check your progress and celebrate your milestones as they arrive!

Are you creating your reality with all life has to offer?

February 16

Today's Self-Love Message:

Always know how much you matter. See the small miracles in each day. Be in awe of how you play a role in the creation of your life. When the world is not what you hoped, you can find comfort in your own heart.

You matter.

February 17

Today's Self-Love Message:

Be the person that you really are and remember who loves you. Experience the joy of each day and be aware of the feelings in your body. Start to make having the life you always wanted a daily practice.

Be thankful for your creation.

February 18

Today's Self-Love Message:

Be in the present moment and allow yourself to experience the bliss that comes with living and breathing each day. Being alive is a miracle.

There is power and peace in your life.

February 19

Today's Self-Love Message:

An internal compass is within you to show the way. It requires effort to be the commander-in-chief of your own contribution to the world. Rise to the occasion and love yourself for all that you are.

You are everlasting bliss.

February 20

Today's Self-Love Message:

Everything is in perfect time. This is the right path. Keep your heart open to this truth.

You will make it to your destination.

February 21

Today's Self-Love Message:

Each day is an opportunity to wake up and be in awe of who you are. You have insurmountable strength to be standing where you are today. Imagine how much further you will carry on.

Be proud of who you are!

February 22

Today's Self-Love Message:

Every day, make a plan to spend 5 minutes doing an activity that brings you joy. Read an article, go for a walk, take a deep breath, or just simply sit. Whatever you can do to give yourself 5 minutes (or more) is worth it.

What will you do today to show the most important
person in your life that you care?

February 23

Today's Self-Love Message:

Create a positive thought bank. During the times when you slip into negative thinking, you can repeat your favorite phrases and shift back into a happier state of mind.

Create more positive moments.

February 24

Today's Self-Love Message:

Some people will misinterpret your messages. When this happens, remember that everyone has his or her own perception. More often than not, people miscommunicate because they are operating in different frequencies. Don't waste time trying to shift another person's point of view. Just continue to establish your belief system. If it is questioned, use that as a sign to learn more about who you present yourself to be.

Practice the power of discernment.

February 25

Today's Self-Love Message:

Speak from your heart and share with others! When you love who you are, people in your life will notice. Show them how important self-care is. This will encourage them to have a strong foundation of it in their life. When you teach your fellow peers about something, it often gives you even more insight for yourself.

Be an expression of love.

February 26

Today's Self-Love Message:

Open the windows to your life and let the new breath of freshness fill your every cell. Be ready for the new space you will create! Let your life be filled with love.

You can create space for more freedom.

February 27

Today's Self-Love Message:

There is beauty in everything that makes up your day-to-day life. Recognize your blessings. Believe in magic. Then watch as a whole new world opens up to you.

You are a miracle!

February 28

Today's Self-Love Message:

It has been said that not everyone will like everyone else; it's just nature's law. Some people will love and others would rather hate. Someone who is mean or unkind, calls names or belittles, will take a major toll on the love you carry for yourself. It causes you to look at what is wrong instead of loving who you are. The only way through this is to keep being who you are. If someone doesn't like you, let it go. Put your energy into the person you are and treat yourself well every chance you get.

Choose to be love.

March

March 1

Today's Self-Love Message:

The love of your life is inside your own heart. Make it a daily practice to always love everything that you are. Cherish the freedom to grow in that love.

Expand your love of self.

March 2

Today's Self-Love Message:

Be flexible with yourself and remember that you are growing every day. Continue to build your greatest potential and direct your thoughts towards what brings you joy. What do you want to see?

See what is real.

March 3

Today's Self-Love Message:

What a liberating feeling to befriend yourself! What a joy it is every day to check in with your own heart! How can you serve yourself today?

Be good to your heart!

March 4

Today's Self-Love Message:

Balance is based upon your own heart's desire in any situation. Love yourself through it all! Stumbling or standing strong, the one constant is you are forever your own best friend.

You are love.

March 5

Today's Self-Love Message:

Love yourself through every motion, whatever it is! Realize in every instance that you are worthy of self-love and compassion.

How will you paint this creation?

March 6

Today's Self-Love Message:

Begin each day by opening your heart to the possibility that lies ahead. Speak words of love into your day. As you begin to create the space for freedom to enjoy life, you will be given all the more reason to keep being free.

You are free!

March 7

Today's Self-Love Message:

Indulge in your own words and love yourself enough to speak truth from your heart. Put all of the focus on accomplishing your dreams because they are possible! This is your story!

Turn toward the light.

March 8

Today's Self-Love Message:

Make the choice every day to love the life you are in. This is the right path. Can you believe in the moment? Can you hold your positive self-image for today? When you give love to yourself, you are able to be more in tune with all life has to offer.

Is there a part of you that could use a little more attention today?

March 9

Today's Self-Love Message:

Be your authentic self. Embrace all of the parts that make you unique and then share all of who you are with your whole heart. In every single way, you are good enough, you are loved, and this is your moment!

Love the parts that make up your whole self.

March 10

Today's Self-Love Message:

Tell yourself every day how important and valuable you are. Thank yourself every morning for arriving at this new day brimming with possibility. Be grateful that this life is your chosen path and you are the person who decided where it would lead. Be proud of all that you have become.

You are divine.

March 11

Today's Self-Love Message:

Be happy with the journey you are on. Remember that the choice is yours and where you are right now is where you thought you should be. Begin with loving who you are today. Then from that place of love ask yourself, what do you need? Listen to the answer your heart gives you.

Listen to your heart's desire and answer its call.

March 12

Today's Self-Love Message:

Accept yourself in every moment. Loving your own self through it all is the only way to be free enough for anyone else to do the same. What does it feel like to be loved? Give it to yourself right now.

You are life.

March 13

Today's Self-Love Message:

Experience life as a continuous flow of energy. Direct your energy with loving awareness and create a more positive experience.

You are on purpose.

March 14

Today's Self-Love Message:

Allow yourself to indulge in the sweetness that you are. Love the place you have come from, appreciate where you stand today, and be ready to navigate your future. Speak words of true empowerment into each day. Believe in yourself and the power you possess.

Listen with your heart.

March 15

Today's Self-Love Message:

You have to open your heart every day to the experiences you encounter in each moment. Stay grounded and believe in the best possible outcome. Love yourself with everything you've got!

You are in the greatest experience!

March 16

Today's Self-Love Message:

Be willing to spend time tending to the cracks in your heart. You have had your love taken for granted, experienced the feelings of great heartache, and have also (more than likely) caused it. In this experience where you are constantly interacting with one another, it is essential to your well-being that you take responsibility for mending, healing, and reopening your own heart. You do this by constantly coming back to your home base, placing your hand over your heart, and genuinely asking what you need. By giving yourself the credit to decide what action is in your best interest, you build self-trust, which in turn allows you to become your #1 most dependable person in life.

You can depend on yourself.

March 17

Today's Self-Love Message:

Create your own luck by believing that even the biggest dreams are possible. They really are! You can do whatever you put your mind to. Have power over your thoughts. This is the best luck you could ever ask for.

You are a lucky person.

March 18

Today's Self-Love Message:

Create small reminders by surrounding yourself with inspiration that resonates with who you really are. Find something every day to celebrate. You are all you need to be.

You are complete.

March 19

Today's Self-Love Message:

What are you able to thank yourself for today? Make a list of your own unique gifts and then bask in the greatness of all that you bring to this life. Be thankful and inspired to share love every day.

Be grateful for yourself.

March 20

Today's Self-Love Message:

Here is to the universe showing you that you are on the right path and the future holds wonderful times ahead. Here is to a day where the love you hold for your own self is amplified to the fullest extent and reflected in those you meet. May you experience respect from colleagues, open doors for new opportunities, and feelings of acceptance. Continue to give yourself love and the opportunity to be happy now.

Love reflects more love.

March 21

Today's Self-Love Message:

Understand that you always have your seasons in life. You work hard and then you are able to watch the effort pay off. In many cases, you do not take the time to stop and acknowledge everything you have become. Take the time today to really feel how much you have accomplished in this life. The ups and downs you have moved through, the heartbreak, the soul mates, the perfect job, the loss of something important, are all intricate details of your story that is still developing. Take the credit you deserve for all that you have created thus far. Then take the reins and guide your life into the next exciting adventure!

You are a never-ending story.

March 22

Today's Self-Love Message:

Listen to your intuition and learn to trust it. What would make you feel better right now? Take the time to listen and keep asking. When you practice this regularly, you begin to develop a deeper sense of self and a forever guide in life. Believe in yourself and trust that everything is unfolding as it should. Celebrate where you are right now; it is such an incredible accomplishment.

You can trust yourself.

March 23

Today's Self-Love Message:

Set an intention today to practice being enough. You are all that you need to be, and you will become all that your heart desires.

You are worthy of everything you want in your life!

March 24

Today's Self-Love Message:

It is about finding common ground. That is where the magic happens. In the journey to self-love, one must find space within that allows for peace—the space where our best intentions and worst nightmare meet, sit down together, and flow in the polarity of one another.

That is balance.

March 25

Today's Self-Love Message:

Be proud of who you are! You are already everything you need to be! You are always on time to where you should be arriving! The better you treat yourself, the more love will show up in your life.

You are the best.

March 26

Today's Self-Love Message:

It is the collective parts of your life that make up the entire expression of who you are. Each intricate detail is not small, but rather an important mark of your design.

Be original.

March 27

Today's Self-Love Message:

What will you focus on today? The way you feel is important and the goal is to keep feeling better and better. Start each day fresh, believe in the possibility of greatness, and hold onto your positive thoughts.

Wonderful things are happening to you every day.

March 28

Today's Self-Love Message:

Sometimes you have to let go and allow the manifestation to occur. Set intentions for what you envision, ask yourself where you want to go, and then release it all to the universe. Believe in the power of positive thinking and relax in the bliss of knowing that it is all coming to you now.

Go where your heart leads you.

March 29

Today's Self-Love Message:

When you love yourself, it is reflected to everyone around you.
Understand and nurture your ability to create the life you want. Love
yourself the way you want others to love you!

You are the reflection of love.

March 30

Today's Self-Love Message:

What if everything was happening in sync with your highest good? How would it feel to imagine that you made all the right choices? You always worry about reaching your goals, doing a certain task, and not missing out, when really everything that you need is open and available. Know that you are on the right path and your life is unfolding as it should.

Be yourself.

March 31

Today's Self-Love Message:

There is no place like coming home to your own heart. Open up to the love you have available for yourself and experience what it is like to be home no matter where you go.

Build a place in your heart that you want to come back to.

April

April 1

Today's Self-Love Message:

It is possible to believe in the best version of yourself with unfaltering faith. Change is a constant pressure in life. People, circumstances, and situations are always going to be in flux. Appreciate the moments that filter in and out of your reality. Accept that things are unable to stay the same and love the time you are in right now!

It is safe to love all that is.

April 2

Today's Self-Love Message:

You do not need to be afraid to let go because you are ready for whatever life brings. You are at peace. You are all that you need to be.

Bring thoughts of love and serenity to your day.

April 3

Today's Self-Love Message:

It is essential to pay attention to the energy you share with others and yourself. Who are the people who feel so right to be around? What is it that makes them interesting and fun to be around? How do you treat yourself--like a sweet friend? Be the person who is good for your own mental health and reflect that loving kindness to everyone else.

You are loved for everything that you are!!

April 4

Today's Self-Love Message:

It is 100% okay to have bad days, to screw everything up, to lose a long hard-fought battle, to say the wrong thing, or to just flat out not care. Still love yourself the same, forgive your humanness, and be ready for whatever the next step brings.

You are enough, you are whole, and you matter!

April 5

Today's Self-Love Message:

Everything exists here in this present moment. You go through your experiences in order to become more of whom you are. This is a process, not a mastery of any kind. It is a way to look at life. You are always a work in progress, may you be content with the idea of never being done.

Your list is filled with love.

April 6

Today's Self-Love Message:

Accept yourself exactly as you are. You are all that you need to be. The world is opening up to you. Everything is happening on time. The challenges make you stronger. Embrace all that is. Love yourself unconditionally.

This is where you need to be.

April 7

Today's Self-Love Message:

When you love someone, they may never leave your heart. If a person is on your mind, then the best thing to do is be honest with yourself and with them. It may be that your story together is not yet finished and there is more to be told. It is possible to fulfill your dreams when you love yourself enough to go after them. You can be honest with how you feel, express your truth, and be okay with whatever comes from that.

Be honest and loving with yourself.

April 8

Today's Self-Love Message:

Trust in what you are being guided to do. You are the person who knows the next best move.

Go for it!

April 9

Today's Self-Love Message:

Believe in the true possibility of joy every day. Happiness can be your constant reality.

You create positive energy.

April 10

Today's Self-Love Message:

When you purposefully listen to your heart, life willingly delivers the best results possible. What would it feel like to have your dreams come true? Imagine it daily and appreciate what has already manifested for you in this moment. Believe it is all real and available to you.

Be on purpose.

April 11

Today's Self-Love Message:

Cherish the moments you have with the people in your life. These times are precious gifts that should be thought of everyday! Even if you are alone, the love that connects you to another is always available in the present moment. Love is the greatest gift. Love transcends all things and it never ends.

Feel the love that others have for you and know how loved you are.

April 12

Today's Self-Love Message:

Believe that your dreams will come true! It is so magical to watch as it all unfolds. Never give up on the passions of your soul.

Believe your dreams into reality.

April 13

Today's Self-Love Message:

Love who you are every day and never forget the importance of the relationship you have with yourself. You are enough, you have all you need, and each day you learn more about who you are.

Trust the process.

April 14

Today's Self-Love Message:

Trust your internal knowing. Give yourself the gift of being your own best friend. Keep moving forward with love for your experience. Your world will completely transform.

You decide your direction.

April 15

Today's Self-Love Message:

Forgive yourself. Holding onto hostility only causes more pain. What can you stop blaming yourself for today? Can you forgive your own mishaps? Can you forgive past decisions that in hindsight could have been handled differently? Yes! It is totally real and possible to give yourself the freedom to be human! Be so in love with yourself that even your most broken parts are recognized as the pieces that make you whole.

Be the complete picture.

April 16

Today's Self-Love Message:

Springtime turns even the most ordinary drive into a magnificent experience. Sometimes places can appear unrecognizable when the blooms of new life begin to open. This sense of renewed growth is a reminder that you are constantly shedding your old self. When you look back with loving forgiveness at the many different places you have been, both emotionally and physically, you almost don't recognize how far you have come. Value the determination it took to get where you are right now.

Give yourself the credit you deserve!

April 17

Today's Self-Love Message:

Each day, remind yourself of how important you are by loving and accepting all that you are.

You are worth the time to be loved.

April 18

Today's Self-Love Message:

You decide how your life will unfold. By positive thinking, changing your thoughts, and believing in the best outcome, you become the greatest version of you!

Love the project that you create by being you.

April 19

Today's Self-Love Message:

How do you love yourself when you are frustrated with the lack of progress you've made? When you feel angry or worthless? How do you love yourself through the biggest disappointment? You tell yourself that you are a continuous work in progress and there is no end goal other than the grand finale of this life. Know that there will always be transitions, moving, changing, and growing. When you comprehend this concept, you will see the value in every single moment of your life. In even the most disappointing times, you can change your perspective. It is always a choice you get to make.

No one in the entire world needs the love
you can give more than you.

April 20

Today's Self-Love Message:

Today is a brand new day that is filled with possibility and surprise. You decide how your day will go. The key to a positive mind is to feel good about yourself. The answers to your questions exist in your own consciousness.

Take the time to listen and nurture your heart today.

April 21

Today's Self-Love Message:

As you grow in self-love, you will bring new people into your life who represent the shift you are making. One major indicator that you have tipped the scale to a more positive life is when people start showing up who have created the life they always wanted. They are the encouragement that you are on the right path. They will remind you of what is possible, and they will often become your new friends. Pay attention to how the world changes when you love who you are more than anything else. Know all is well. Love exists inside of you and the universe is ready for you.

You are so appreciated.

April 22

Today's Self-Love Message:

Be blessed by the people in your life. All experiences bring more truth about who you are. See each relationship as an opportunity to grow in loving compassion for yourself and those who are a part of your world.

Fill your life up with joy.

April 23

Today's Self-Love Message:

Appreciate all that you do to take care of yourself and everyone else who depends on you. Be sure to take time each day to be thankful for you!

Do something that is just for you as a sign of your self-appreciation.

April 24

Today's Self-Love Message:

Know that the universe wants you to accomplish your dreams. In order to be successful, you have to love what you are creating. Meet each step of the journey with an open heart.

Reflect love and be open to receive.

April 25

Today's Self-Love Message:

Communication is so very important to the overall well-being of the human soul. You want to be heard, to feel valued, and give a worthy response. It is normal to feel personally attacked when people are unable to understand the message you are sharing. Self-love means knowing that all you can do is express what is in your heart, share it with whoever is listening, and believe that the message will get to the person who needs to hear it. Do you listen and give yourself the attention that you seek from other people? Take the time today to communicate with yourself.

Love who you are and feel that love in return.

April 26

Today's Self-Love Message:

Enjoy the process of becoming who you are with each step of your journey. Understand that instant gratification is always available to you when you realize in this moment you have it all. Give the universe permission to continue providing for you. Show up each day with gratitude. Trust that what you desire will come to you. Check in to be sure that what you are thinking about is what you want to manifest into your present reality.

Thoughts become your life.

April 27

Today's Self-Love Message:

When you love yourself, life opens up all the possibilities you have been waiting for. Love yourself every day, no matter what. It is a necessary part of the unique story you are creating. Love yourself through every step of your journey.

Manifest your greatest potential.

April 28

Today's Self-Love Message:

Trusting that you are in the right place at the right time can be difficult. Be open to accept what is. Having a good day is not decided by the circumstances, it is in how you tell the story. No doubt it is hard to see the other side of a hard day, but there is always a positive decision that can be made. When you take the time to improve your thoughts, the universe responds accordingly. Even when another test arrives, the more you practice the art of positive perspective, the more it becomes your natural response.

Practice positive responses.

April 29

Today's Self-Love Message:

In every moment, you are planting the seeds of your future reality. You literally water and grow your dreams. Each person has the power within him or her to create the greatest possible outcome. What will you pay attention to today?

Every moment is a precious gift.

April 30

Today's Self-Love Message:

The divine intervention you seek outside of yourself is always alive in you. The root cause of any disconnect can be resolved by taking the time to listen to your heart. Go to that wounded place and love it for what it has taught you. Then watch as the love for who you are grows anew.

Stand strong.

May

May 1

Today's Self-Love Message:

Loving yourself and having compassion through every circumstance is the only answer. What can you begin to let go of? What can you do to help your own spirit be free of what no longer serves you? The answer is within.

Listen and respond to your heart.

May 2

Today's Self-Love Message:

Love what you have created. Take credit for how far you have come. Always know that the next step is the right one for you at this time.

Believe in your own guidance.

May 3

Today's Self-Love Message:

You deserve to be content, experience joy, and have a fulfilling life. Abundance, happiness, and positivity are natural life occurrences that you always have access to. Remind yourself to find courage and confidence within. You are ready for whatever life brings.

Expect greatness.

May 4

Today's Self-Love Message:

Always know your worth. This is not a value anyone else can give you. You are worthy of the life you most desire. Go into the world today wearing your worthiness like a crown. You are worthy of peace, promise, prosperity, health, and happiness.

Let it be yours.

May 5

Today's Self-Love Message:

Love is available to each of you. Be open to your experience and love every part of it.

Love is who you are.

May 6

Today's Self-Love Message:

Love this life and its possibilities! You never know what exciting adventure can happen. The world is your playground! Go experience it!

What is your favorite way to play?

May 7

Today's Self-Love Message:

When troubles arise or anxious thoughts race through your head, take control of your breath. This will help you arrive here in this present moment space. Trust the process.

Make it simple and make it happen!

May 8

Today's Self-Love Message:

It takes time to be okay with yourself when you are going through life changes, tough circumstances, or leaps of faith. You are on a journey that has been set to the beat of your own natural rhythm. Sometimes you need to be lifted up by something bigger than yourself. Help is out there and you can ask for it whenever you need more support.

Receive and return the favor.

May 9

Today's Self-Love Message:

Trust your own instinct. Know that you are fully capable of making the best choice for your own life. If you doubt who you are, the world will do the same. Check in and ask what your whole self (mind/body/soul) wants to create. Build yourself with love.

Release and rebuild!

May 10

Today's Self-Love Message:

Things do not always go as planned, no matter how hard you try to make them happen. Rather than breakdown, keep refocusing on what it is that you really want. Release the grip you have on controlling the outcome. Everything is always working out the way it should.

You are one with your destiny.

May 11

Today's Self-Love Message:

One thing is always guaranteed in life, and that is change. Life circumstances will shift, and people will come and go. Sometimes this happens without any warning. Just think of all of the possibilities of change. It may be in your job, your surroundings, friendships, or family dynamics; even the outdoor scenery shifts on a daily basis. In order to find grounding in a world of transitions, accept that change is your stability.

Each path is unique.

May 12

Today's Self-Love Message:

Whether it is a Monday or a Friday, life is a blessing, and you have so much to be thankful for. Set an intention for gratitude and positivity, then envision these gifts permeating your entire day. Spend time getting to know what makes you happy and make a promise to do it at least once a week.

Manifest the life you have always wanted.

May 13

Today's Self-Love Message:

Let go of control. Release the iron grip of how it must be and let what is supposed to happen flow freely.

This is what allowing feels like.

May 14

Today's Self-Love Message:

Being born on this earth is such an incredible miracle. It is an invitation to live the best version of who you are. You are here to appreciate the perfection that you co-create with the universe. Celebrate life today and be thankful for the people who have carved a space for you on this journey.

Be blessed with each breath you take.

May 15

Today's Self-Love Message:

You are a work in progress, and this work is never done. The time you spend investing in what makes you happy is the best way to use your energy. How you feel about yourself is what you bring to the table for everyone else. Start with loving who you are every day; it is the most important part to being alive!

Be in love with yourself.

May 16

Today's Self-Love Message:

Love yourself enough to follow your heart! Even if what you dream about seems unattainable, continue to be a self-motivator. Loving yourself means taking action towards your goal. When opportunities for action arise, let them serve as a calling to step into who you are meant to be.

Believe in who you are.

May 17

Today's Self-Love Message:

See the colors in the world and appreciate the sweet consistency of life. What can you promise to do every day to keep your focus on the positive?

Have a great day.

May 18

Today's Self-Love Message:

Your point of view is the basis and foundation of how your story is told. There may be times when you feel like you need to correct the person that you are. Start to believe that you are whole and complete right now. You are perfect and so much more than you even realize.

Respond to life with positivity.

May 19

Today's Self-Love Message:

Friends are so important! As you share your love and connect with others, your own ability to love grows ever stronger. Keep reaching into your own heart to be your own friend and then share yourself with others along the way.

Connect with the people who have joined you on this journey.

May 20

Today's Self-Love Message:

Taking care of yourself is a way of showing gratitude to all that you have been given in this life. Take the time to relish in all that you are. What does your self-care look like? Love yourself and evolve each day.

Be thankful.

May 21

Today's Self-Love Message:

Make a promise to yourself every day for the rest of this year. What is one simple thing you can do that makes you happy? In making this simple commitment, you build trust and open up to happiness. Loving yourself is a daily task of honoring who you are and taking the time to nurture yourself first. When you serve your soul, you open up so much more to the world around you.

Express your joy in being here by doing what makes you happy.

May 22

Today's Self-Love Message:

What does loving you look like? How does it feel? How do you need to be shown love? If you cannot answer these questions, you will be unable to give or receive love fully. Take time this week to write down what loving you means. Then from that place of self-love, discover how you receive love from others.

What makes you feel loved?

May 23

Today's Self-Love Message:

Some days it is hard to be appreciative and receptive to the journey. What if, instead of trying to change your feelings, you just accepted what is? Once you are able to be present for your emotions, the space is made for shifting the focus to a solution. Take the time to recuperate from any challenging situation and your peace will return.

It is a good day to do something completely different.

May 24

Today's Self-Love Message:

Take care of yourself and do what you love. Be proud of how far you have come and reward yourself for all that you do! It is so important to fill up on what makes you happy!

Remember how much you are loved.

May 25

Today's Self-Love Message:

Be on this path with an open heart and continue to embrace each moment. Remember to breathe and let the gift of life bless you!

Open up and receive.

May 26

Today's Self-Love Message:

Believe in your dreams coming true! Follow your intuition and have faith that this journey will be all that you could ever imagine. Let go of controlling how all of this will happen and just know it is possible.

Listen to the call of your heart.

May 27

Today's Self-Love Message:

Relax and enjoy the simple things in life. Every day you go through many different experiences. Allow yourself time to renew in-between the passing moments. You deserve to be here and to love this life!

Find your happiness in a daily practice of self-love.

May 28

Today's Self-Love Message:

Spend time with the people you love because that is what matters.
Be present for them, enjoy the memories, and receive the love given
to you in return!

Your time is a gift.

May 29

Today's Self-Love Message:

Be ready for the gifts as they come into your life. Ask for what you need, be open to receive, and allow the outcome to surprise you. Let love be your guiding force and watch as the world opens up to you.

Respond to life with a smile and watch as it smiles back at you.

May 30

Today's Self-Love Message:

Share your talents and be open to receive guidance from others. Have appreciation for the people in your life who offer outside perspective. You are a gift! It is a good idea to let yourself be reminded of that from the people who love you.

Thank you for being here!

May 31

Today's Self-Love Message:

Never give up on your dreams, even if they seem to be passing you by. It is not always easy to believe that everything happens for a reason. Be steadfast on your path and know you will always reach your destination!

Each step is in the right direction.

June

June 1

Today's Self-Love Message:

What are you going to do with this life? Wish that things were better or different? Instead of wishing, take action! Gather facts and move forward with whatever your heart guides you to do.

Life is magical.

June 2

Today's Self-Love Message:

Love who you are and have a grateful heart. This is your journey and you should be enjoying the ride! Whichever direction the detours of free will may take you, know that you will be prepared and have everything you need. Keep your mind open to the endless possibility that each day holds.

Spend time listening to your inner self.

June 3

Today's Self-Love Message:

When something wonderful happens, write it down and acknowledge the positive experience. Allow more of what you desire into your life. Release the outcome and focus on loving who you are. Surrender to the experience and trust that everything will be taken care of.

Acknowledge what you want more of.

June 4

Today's Self-Love Message:

Trust that your passion in life has a purpose. Know that each step is divinely guided in order to support your greatest evolvement. Desire the outcome you are longing for and believe that it will happen.

Have absolute faith in the best possible outcome.

June 5

Today's Self-Love Message:

Focus on gratitude and positivity. Your job is to keep thinking better and better thoughts. It is a daily commitment, but it is the best one you will ever make!

Be mindful of your thoughts.

June 6

Today's Self-Love Message:

It is time to forgive yourself for any guilt you are carrying. Life is what you make it. Sometimes you have to try out a new way of living in order to understand who you are in a more profound way. In paving your path, you might make mistakes, hurt people, or just simply act out in a way that is untrue to your real self. Many times, you focus on the error instead of seeing it as a way to learn and move on. This is why you stay stuck, and it is time to break free! Let go of guilt. When your mind starts to list reasons otherwise, remember you are the force behind what you listen to, believe, or engage in. Tell your thoughts of guilt that you love and accept yourself. That you understand mistakes happen in life. Forgive those who have brought confusion, disorder, and pain. Rejoice in being alive- no matter who you are- you are still just learning how to be the best version of yourself.

What can you let go of today? What words of peace can you offer to your soul?

Forgive so you can be free from suffering.

June 7

Today's Self-Love Message:

What if everything you wanted came to you with ease? What would that feel like? Think about what the word ease means to you. Suspend any worry or difficulty. Just see yourself there, notice everything you can about what it means to you, and allow for it to be easy.

Let what you want come to you with ease.

June 8

Today's Self-Love Message:

Cherish the moments that make up the story of your life. Appreciate the valuable friendships, families, and communities that are here for you in this experience. Speak up for who you are. Create a space that honors the truth of who you are. Focus on your dreams and be present for each of the steps you have taken along the way.

Cherish every part of that which makes you whole.

June 9

Today's Self-Love Message:

No matter what the experiences are, they come and go. If you spent a day writing down your most prevalent thoughts, you would see the example of them in your real-world perspective. If you want to change what is happening, all it takes is shifting your mind.

Hope can be a forward moving action.

June 10

Today's Self-Love Message:

In all that you have become, what is your favorite thing about being you? When you find the answer, incorporate more of it into your daily life. You know what is best for your own personal self-care.

What serves your highest purpose?

June 11

Today's Self-Love Message:

Experience and accept yourself for exactly who you are. Make a commitment to focus on how you will manifest your truest desires. You are free and perfect. Trust your intuition and know that everything is unfolding as it should.

Live your life purpose.

June 12

Today's Self-Love Message:

Sometimes, when it is so hard to maintain happiness, the only thing to do is embrace the pain. Befriend it, find out where the core suffering is coming from, and then begin to nurture your heart back to health. You can't always be your best, but you can always give yourself the best you have in each moment. That's what self-love is, loving who you are through it all!!

Spend time healing and nurturing your heart.

June 13

Today's Self-Love Message:

Release the ideas you hold onto that say this life is not what you intended it to be. When you have struggled for a long time, it is hard to appreciate what is going right. Reprogram the unsupportive messages of your mind to be in a state of gratitude, love, and receptivity. Allow for more of what you really want into your life.

Listen to your calling.

June 14

Today's Self-Love Message:

Rest when you are weary, it is a necessary part of self-care. If you are worn out, it is going to be nearly impossible to accomplish big tasks. Listen to yourself and take a break. Once you have honored your body, the energy will be replenished to complete your to-do list. Remember the major events you work on never stop. One check off the list just means you have created space for more tasks to be added. Enjoy the process.

Rest is a wise use of time.

June 15

Today's Self-Love Message:

The moment you realize that you are indeed a divine being, the world begins to change. This isn't a competition to see which person gets there the fastest or works on themselves the most. This is an internal relationship that begins with a promise to be still and listen to your own unique message from your inner knowing self. Trust this, befriend your soul, and be a blessing to yourself every day. What is your soul's message? Listen, inquire within, and be open to what you are able to learn about the most important person in the world! That's you!

Spend time with your built-in best friend.

June 16

Today's Self-Love Message:

When you value all of who you are, the world reflects worthiness back to you. Be your own most prized possession. The acceptance you seek from the outside world must come from you first. Think positive, pray for release, and believe that you are worthy of the greatest version of your life.

In time, all that you want will be yours.

June 17

Today's Self-Love Message:

Love with all of your heart and light up the world. Be so in love with yourself that you are able to be your own caretaker. Be the light that you are! You are needed exactly as you are destined to be.

Open and expand your life to the fullest expression.

June 18

Today's Self-Love Message:

Breathe in and out. Experience the miracle of this action you take all the time. It is the reason you are able to sustain life on this planet. Take several moments to acknowledge this powerful connection to all life on this earth. You are a part of the greater consciousness.

Share awareness every day.

June 19

Today's Self-Love Message:

Looking to outside sources for peace or approval will leave you feeling depleted, depressed, and empty. You have enough within you to create any kind of reality you are seeking. Shine light on the darkness; let your experiences bring you even closer to your own heart. Ask yourself daily how to serve your own purpose and be amazed as you receive what it is you seek. In the entire world, the only place you can find yourself is in your heart!

You are enough and capable of all things.

June 20

Today's Self-Love Message:

Be present and grateful for all of life's experiences. This is your chance to be great, and you get to decide what that means to you. Go be who you always said you would be one day. You have everything you need and then some!

You are happening right now.

June 21

Today's Self-Love Message:

You have so many stored memories in your bones. Whether the experience was good or bad, you internalize it as part of your muscle memory. Go get a massage, take a salt bath, and treat your body to a healing session! Renew your body and soul.

Release everything that does not serve your highest calling.

June 22

Today's Self-Love Message:

Love yourself with all that you've got. Do not question your worth.
Everything you desire is available to you.

Happiness is a natural part of life.

June 23

Today's Self-Love Message:

Love yourself so much that you allow everything you ever wanted to be yours. Live as if all of your wishes were your reality. Believe it and it will be yours!

Your thoughts manifest your reality.

June 24

Today's Self-Love Message:

It can be difficult to master control of your attention when you have so many things to accomplish. Look at what is ahead of you and decide how to best serve your purpose. Appreciate your gifts and honor them individually. Pick a passion, follow your intuition, and focus your energy on what you want to manifest.

Use your energy wisely and with purpose.

June 25

Today's Self-Love Message:

Believe and know that anything is possible. Keep your intention focused on what you want and then allow the experiences to enter your life. Realize that without a doubt you are in exact alignment with everything you seek. You deserve it and are worthy.

Give yourself credit!

June 26

Today's Self-Love Message:

Be you no matter where you are. You are love! Always remember that the world needs you and that you are so very loved. Always know how valuable you are!

Love is around you.

June 27

Today's Self-Love Message:

Happiness is a choice you make every day. The feeling of pure joy is always available.

Believe and it will come to you.

June 28

Today's Self-Love Message:

Take time to rest and rejuvenate your soul. Slow down. Notice the world around you. Find peace in knowing everything is working out perfectly.

Rest in your worth.

June 29

Today's Self-Love Message:

You are a divine being filled with the highest potential. Success is yours, and whatever you seek is available to you. Keep going! Stay focused on your goal and watch as the perceived blocks become stepping-stones to your dreams coming true!

You are filled with all the potential you can imagine and more.

June 30

Today's Self-Love Message:

You are incredible! Always be kind to yourself. Always know how much you are loved.

Step into the life you have with love.

July

July 1

Today's Self-Love Message:

Relax and allow life to happen. Move through life knowing all that you desire is available to you. The more you confidently believe in yourself, the more you are able to manifest immediately.

Allowing is aligning with possibility.

July 2

Today's Self-Love Message:

Open up to love! It's all around you in every moment. All you have to do is believe and receive it. Then continue to let it be your driving force. Love is everything and with it you can do anything.

How does being loved make you feel?

July 3

Today's Self-Love Message:

Love yourself - especially the parts you want to change. Everything grows better when it is showered with love.

Give yourself love and watch it grow.

July 4

Today's Self-Love Message:

Set an intention every day before you do anything else. Believe that you have the power to direct your life in the way you want it to go. Everything is tied to whatever you focus on the most. Make sure your thoughts are in alignment with your greatest purpose.

It's your choice to experience bliss.

July 5

Today's Self-Love Message:

Loving yourself is being in the moment. Accept all that you are and never leave a part of yourself out of the picture. Decide that you are capable of recognizing all that you are as a gift.

Open up to this moment.

July 6

Today's Self-Love Message:

When you look at life from a perspective of love, you are able to see how every part matters to the experience. Choose to see the battles and victories as both serving a purpose.

Be all of who you are.

July 7

Today's Self-Love Message:

Express who you are. Love those around you and love yourself. Allow the process of loving yourself to be something you look forward to. Be excited to treat yourself well every day of your life!

Love it all.

July 8

Today's Self-Love Message:

Give credit to your journey and reach out for more of what you seek in this current reality. Transforming yourself is only possible if you can find purpose in everything you are. Love your whole self and accept the gift you have in this life.

Give yourself credit for the contributions you make.

July 9

Today's Self-Love Message:

How often do you take the time in your day to send gratitude? Create space to honor your life and allow for more positivity to flow in.

Be thankful.

July 10

Today's Self-Love Message:

Take time to grow. Be in your body, experience life, and appreciate the person who you have become.

Discover new parts of yourself.

July 11

Today's Self-Love Message:

Ride the wave of your greatest potential. Release your control, wait for your guidance to move, and trust in the perfect timing of everything. Whatever you desire is yours. Enjoy watching as your greatest reality unfolds.

Trust and have faith in your destiny.

July 12

Today's Self-Love Message:

Love is such a gift to share with others and most of all to give to our own hearts. Believe in the power of love and let it be your guiding force. If you operate with love, the world will reflect the same back to you. Be the love you seek from others and let it flow to you with ease.

What is the best way to receive love?

July 13

Today's Self-Love Message:

How quickly you arrive at your destination is up to you. The only thing keeping you closed off is your own fear. Be okay with the idea that things are happening at the pace you decide. Then when you are ready for more, you can create the space you need to expand.

You are always using your own free will.

July 14

Today's Self-Love Message:

Believe in yourself and have the courage to stand up and be you! It might be scary, but all you need to do is have faith that the universe is working to accomplish the desires of your heart.

The belief of your own self is everything.

July 15

Today's Self-Love Message:

There are so many factors when working with manifesting your dreams. Other people may want the same thing. The offer might not be available or the timing is off. Sometimes the thing you want the most is what seems to be the farthest from your reach. It is so disappointing to not get what you want. So how do you let go of that bitter feeling?

Change your perspective and believe that life lessons are the path to wisdom. You will get to wherever you are meant to be because it is only available to you. Believe that every no you receive means it was out of alignment from the place where you would be the happiest. Then step back out and play the game again. Never give up.

It is your choice to decide how you react to your life experience.

July 16

Today's Self-Love Message:

How will you contribute to your life through love? Can you see all the different ways in which you express love? Sharing love has a ripple effect. The physical and nonphysical expressions of love make being here an even more joyous event.

Be the love and spread it wherever you go.

July 17

Today's Self-Love Message:

When you talk to yourself, when you speak with others, and when you are nonverbally communicating with the universe, what is your message? Are you bringing higher frequencies in or are you lowering yourself to meet the expectations of others? In order to reach a place of contentment, you have to take the time to weed out negative influences in your life. Eat healthy, vibrant foods, spend time in nature, listen to motivational speakers, read uplifting books, listen to music that speaks joy to your heart, and most of all do these things with gratitude. Be the light and surround yourself with all that is good.

You are the energy you put out and the energy you get back.

July 18

Today's Self-Love Message:

Every day you are tuned to a frequency. Associate with people who are filled with light. Move away from the things/people/places that make you feel anything less than your best self. Frequency is your choice. What are you tuning into?

Keep your positive vibration strong.

July 19

Today's Self-Love Message:

Self-love starts in the morning by sending gratitude to your life. It is a way to create more things to be grateful for.

It starts and ends with you.

July 20

Today's Self-Love Message:

Send gratitude for the signs that show up all around you as reminders of what it is you are manifesting in this life. Be grateful to all that is here in your journey. This is your gift. Be present for this life and all that is dear to you.

Be on purpose.

July 21

Today's Self-Love Message:

Be thankful for how many people you are lucky to know. Recall all of the beautiful places you have visited. This is such a magical world to live in and it is filled with endless possibilities.

All of the time and resources are available.

July 22

Today's Self-Love Message:

You have a lot going on all the time. How you use your time in this life is very important to your overall happiness. When your heart is open to experience everything in life, all of your tasks become miniature meditations. Always be willing to do whatever it takes to keep sharing your gift with the world! Work for what you love!

Live your life on purpose.

July 23

Today's Self-Love Message:

You have it all and you are never without. Find inner strength and trust in yourself. Realize how once you connect with who you really are, everything else just opens up to you. Be what you are seeking from outside of you. Then it will unmistakably know how to find you in every moment.

Call upon yourself to manifest the life you seek.

July 24

Today's Self-Love Message:

You are such a bright and beautiful being! When you are fully engaged with your authentic self, you bring people into your life who share your same frequency. Look at what is present right now and decide if you are open to your highest vibration.

Let your light shine.

July 25

Today's Self-Love Message:

Arrange your thoughts like a bouquet of flowers. Optimal placement, careful consideration, and precise pruning will bring the most fulfilling results.

Keep your thoughts beautiful.

July 26

Today's Self-Love Message:

You are guided every day by your higher knowing self, the spiritual soul. Develop your intuition by paying attention to your daily intentions. Listen to what you are saying to yourself. Get to know the observer that is your divine connection.

Befriend your spirit.

July 27

Today's Self-Love Message:

Take time out to rejuvenate yourself. Sometimes it is just needed for a brief period, while other breaks last longer. It's okay to need rest and solitude. These are the moments where you really get to know yourself. Be still so that you can hear the whispers of your soul.

Quiet moments of reflection are necessary.

July 28

Today's Self-Love Message:

How have you decorated the things in your life? The space you occupy is a reflection of who you are and how you are feeling. Be mindful of your surroundings. Consciously work to reflect your highest good by expressing goodness in all that you do.

Clean out and refresh.

July 29

Today's Self-Love Message:

Always be kind to yourself in every moment. When doing daily tasks, ask yourself if you're performing them with attention. When you use your thoughts to generate positive energy towards all that you do, you get more in return. A very easy way to do this is tuning into your thoughts every day while you do whatever it is that is on the schedule. Be grateful for all that is happening right now because it is temporary.

Do all things with kindness.

July 30

Today's Self-Love Message:

Check your mind chatter frequently and make a conscious effort to focus on thoughts that serve your purpose. Sort through your thoughts and create the intention to live a more magical life.

Be mindful and listen.

July 31

Today's Self-Love Message:

Friends are an important part of this journey. They bring companionship, love, memories, and good times with them. When you meet a friend, it feels good because you share similarities with them. Friends are your frequency reflected back to you. You will all go through different phases in your life. Friends are the people who can remind you of how far you have come and how to get back to your own heart if you have lost your way.

Love the people in your life.

August

August 1

Today's Self-Love Message:

It always works out. That's what it does. Your perception is the experience you are having. Decide what you want and then be on the way to your happiest life.

Be you.

August 2

Today's Self-Love Message:

No matter what happens, you must keep going and believing in yourself. You are experiencing this life and you know how to move forward. When something throws you off balance, let go! You don't need to make excuses for the way others behave. All you have to do is be your own true authentic self. Spend time in the quiet ocean of your heart. Listen to the messages of love that you receive.

When you are confused, seek inner guidance.

August 3

Today's Self-Love Message:

Keep going and don't let the end goal keep you from seeing the value of each mile on this journey. It's easy to forget how far you have come. Be grateful for the pauses in action and take stock in all that you have already accomplished. The road never ends; it just gets bigger the more you travel.

You have arrived.

August 4

Today's Self-Love Message:

Carry your love with you wherever you go. Encourage your steps when they feel less than accurate, and remind yourself the path is available through several trails. You are not always going to walk with those who you hold dearest, but you will love forever. That is how you hold the world in your hands, by loving it even as it passes away.

Love with all that you have.

August 5

Today's Self-Love Message:

You have climbed many mountains, some without any support. You are capable of working with what is available and making it into exactly what you need. When you feel like something is missing, look closer because the solutions are alive inside of you. When you reach a plateau, rest and enjoy how much you have accomplished.

Climb your mountain.

August 6

Today's Self-Love Message:

Believe in your passion because it is what you are supposed to do. When you tune into your heart's desire, the world provides multiple opportunities to express who you really are. Be thankful for the ability to share your gift and to receive abundance in return.

You are the light!

August 7

Today's Self-Love Message:

Loving yourself through all that you experience each day is a gift to your heart that no other person can give you. There is a sea of love inside you, greater than anything you can experience outside of yourself.

Your heart is a safe place to come back to!

August 8

Today's Self-Love Message:

You pick up so many different feelings in a day. Be sure that you are not holding onto something that weighs you down, makes you sad, or feels wrong because it belongs to someone else. You can always check in, release what is not yours, and then check again to see if you feel better. You have control over your energy, emotions, and how you respond to life circumstances. Honor that power by treating yourself well, loving who you are, and reflecting what you want the world to see.

Return to your own energy.

August 9

Today's Self-Love Message:

You are always on time! There are no late arrivals, early dismissals, or missed opportunities in this life. Be in the present moment and allow what you need to be magnetically drawn to your timeline.

Open up to every opportunity.

August 10

Today's Self-Love Message:

The only way to stay balanced is to keep moving forward. The point of focus is what keeps you from falling off the path. No matter what external forces show up, continue to persevere. Be stronger than the winds that make you sway. Know that as long as you keep going, you will be successful in all that you set your intention on accomplishing.

Keep the momentum going.

August 11

Today's Self-Love Message:

The label you assign to the events and circumstances in your life become your reward. For example, do you say that something is hard or do you say it's a learning experience? You learn a lot about yourself when you listen to the thoughts in your head that seem to run on autopilot. This is actually one of your most valuable tools, the power of positive, habitual thinking!! Harness this gift! Label your life according to your highest good.

Make it a habit to think positive thoughts.

August 12

Today's Self-Love Message:

Each step is essential to your story. Take everything you have learned and apply it to the path that you are walking. What other people say is not as important. Stay true to your own unique spirit.

Follow the staircase to your destiny.

August 13

Today's Self-Love Message:

Forgiveness is a gift you can offer to yourself in the face of all adversity. You can forgive yourself for making mistakes. You are here to learn and experience life, not carry guilt or shame. Forgiveness of others allows you to stand proud in who you are. When you accept your own truth, no one can deter you from that place of inner peace. It is time to fully let go, without fear, of all that no longer serves you. Forgiveness is the path to releasing past bondages and being okay with never going back to that space again. Forgive yourself and believe that in doing so you are free!

There is always more to life.

August 14

Today's Self-Love Message:

Love yourself will all that you have! It is a daily task to wake up in love with who you are right now. Self-love means accepting all that your life encompasses. It means believing in your own journey more than any other person does. Use your energy to uplift everything around you. Trust that what is destined to be yours is available right now. Believe in your worth. Trust that the universe is conspiring right now to make all of your dreams come true!

It is possible to have it all.

August 15

Today's Self-Love Message:

Do everything from the light because that is what you are. Allow your heart to guide you and make every decision from a place of love. There are many ways you can recognize the miracle of being alive. Every day, ask your heart for guidance and send gratitude out into the world. What are you thankful for? What does love feel like? Can you share your light with everyone today?

Know that all is well.

August 16

Today's Self-Love Message:

You are never stuck in life. Think of a river being blocked by a buildup of debris. Somehow the river will eventually overcome the obstacle. Life is similar. Slowing down is often a signal to rearrange what you already have. Free yourself by going in a new direction.

Move forward with your life.

August 17

Today's Self-Love Message:

The other side of letting go is happiness.

It is that simple.

August 18

Today's Self-Love Message:

Adjusting to your feelings after letting go can be exhausting from time to time. Just continue to be clear on your intentions and know that all is well. Ask yourself how to be more open to the present experience for your highest good right now!

Your heart is your home.

August 19

Today's Self-Love Message:

The story of your life is your perception of what has happened. As you become more aware of your thoughts and actions, you will see how much control you have in creating the life you always wanted. If what you want and where you are seem impossibly far from each other, remember everything is always changing. If you are ready for a new possibility, you have to be open to seeing your life from a different point of view.

This is only right now.

August 20

Today's Self-Love Message:

Freedom is opening your heart to all that is available to you. Forgive your heart for it has been through many trials and deserves to be acknowledged. No matter what has happened, just keep opening to each experience. Be assured that nothing is ever wasted. You have the capacity to keep going, and you are never alone.

Support and love everything about you.

August 21

Today's Self-Love Message:

Understand that the light will always come through even when you can't see it. When a seed is planted, it is covered by soil and submerged into complete darkness. Even still, the seed feels the warmth of the sun. It knows that it contains the power of life within itself. Everything you seek is within your own soul. Keep your light burning and trust that you are growing exactly as you should.

In the darkness, you can always recall the light.

August 22

Today's Self-Love Message:

If you only focus on how others perceive you, then you spend your precious time on earth letting someone else tell you how to live! Know yourself well enough to stay focused on what is best for you!

Be your true self.

August 23

Today's Self-Love Message:

Life always keeps moving. You are waiting to see how far you will go. Learn from each experience and trust what is unfolding. The time to celebrate is right now. You are at the top of your game, keep going!

You are safe and secure.

August 24

Today's Self-Love Message:

Precious memories are always with you. It is normal to feel sad when these moments of bliss come to an end. Next time you are having a perfect day, remind yourself that there will always be more. Every day will be magical if you allow it to be.

Making memories is a daily occurrence.

August 25

Today's Self-Love Message:

Your thinking patterns directly affect how you are feeling. Be free of judgment and release everything that no longer serves your purpose. When you are ready, everything will fall into place.

You are not alone.

August 26

Today's Self-Love Message:

Circumstances and events may have cost you everything and left you coming up short, but you kept going! The reward is your transformation! You are here to serve a higher purpose with the unique gifts you offer. Use what you were made to do for something meaningful.

It is a good time to be you.

August 27

Today's Self-Love Message:

Respond to life as an open-hearted, kind, and loving soul. The world needs more happy people walking around.

Reflect happiness to everyone you encounter.

August 28

Today's Self-Love Message:

You exist in this massive space that has so much opportunity for your life. Loving who you are means accepting that not everyone swims with your kind of class. Keep being the soul that you are, find your peace, and don't let anything or anyone take it from you.

Keep returning to your natural state of bliss.

August 29

Today's Self-Love Message:

Inner strength is something you develop over time. You light up the world when you express your compassion for life. Be kind to those around you and be the best version of yourself every day. Show up and make a difference, be respectful of others, and give life all you have!

Give it your all and trust the outcome.

August 30

Today's Self-Love Message:

You never know the places you may go until you take the steps to move in that direction. Decide what that means and set your intention to go for it! Let it be the manifestation of all your dreams coming true.

Expand your dreams.

August 31

Today's Self-Love Message:

Being alone and really knowing who you are takes dedication. It means being open to have everything you thought you knew about yourself exposed over and over again. It means still being able to love these new versions of you, especially when the facts and players change. Be proud of who you are and know you will always go further.

It is all about what you do.

September

September 1

Today's Self-Love Message:

Home is here. This beautiful and miraculous earth is your home. How you feel about yourself emits a strong energy. You have the capacity to be and do whatever you want. What do you want to contribute to this existence?

It is your right to be happy and love who you are.

September 2

Today's Self-Love Message:

Stay in the experience, breathe through the emotions, and utilize the tools available for your mental health. This is all a part of the process. When you are able to hold space for all that you experience, you can keep your sanity even when you feel the world closing in. Present moment peace is always available. Find the place of peace inside yourself.

Be in that space.

September 3

Today's Self-Love Message:

Intuition grows with attention. Listen and act on your inner guidance to learn more about your personal connection to spirit. Find out what it feels like to listen to your heart's calling and act on your passions. You are powerful. Honor your gift.

Be open to receive in all that you do!

September 4

Today's Self-Love Message:

Steps are the way to success. You have to be willing to climb when it's time to move up. Know that when life seems to knock the wind out of you, it is only because you are transforming into your upgraded self. Imagine that every hardship has been a growth process. Expand upward from your past and reach for greater heights.

Inner strength is in your soul.

September 5

Today's Self-Love Message:

Continue to keep moving and believing in yourself. You are working through these different paths to reach your tribe of people. That's the beauty of it all.

The magic of the world surrounds you.

September 6

Today's Self-Love Message:

When you are meant to do something, you can feel it! The body has a lot to offer as a way of knowing what is right or wrong. Check in and feel the response when you are moving throughout your day. Take the time to care for the body you live in.

Connect to your heart before speaking your mind.

September 7

Today's Self-Love Message:

Love is all that you are. Fill up on your own self- worth! See your own reflection of self-love in the people you meet. Dedicate your effort to loving yourself more. You are so important.

You bring value to the entire world.

September 8

Today's Self-Love Message:

Peace and love are within you. Breathe in the truth and exhale all that does not support your highest good. Be thankful for all that you have.

Open up to the experience.

September 9

Today's Self-Love Message:

Wake up and be here. Do what makes you feel happy! Be amazed at the small wonders that happen to you every day. It's all about perception, patience, and acceptance. Accept that you are where you are because this is what you manifested. Be grateful for whatever is happening. Choose to see the beauty in every circumstance.

You are here because you chose to be.

September 10

Today's Self-Love Message:

Value your time and do not worry. When you plan your life to be a joyous journey, it will meet your expectations! Joy will bring the light of all that you desire into your most present reality.

Ride your rollercoaster and enjoy the thrill.

September 11

Today's Self-Love Message:

Balance is floating between surrender and trust. Believe in your heart. Listen to the wisdom of your spirit. Be easy on yourself.

All is well.

September 12

Today's Self-Love Message:

Be so in love with yourself that you allow the shedding of anything that does not serve your highest good to be released. Tune into what you need the most.

Be authentic.

September 13

Today's Self-Love Message:

When you are ready to move on, the path will appear. Letting go isn't always easy. It can be gruesome and filled with tears. Trust that what you are seeking is reaching out to you and just waiting for you to take that step. Be your own warrior and step up to the next level!

The time is now.

September 14

Today's Self-Love Message:

Inside your heart is the answer to who you are. Start there and then check in with the mind to see if it agrees. Keep working until the heart and mind can settle on what it is. The sign that you have uncovered a personal truth is that you will feel it in your body. Relax and accept all that is coming.

You are always with yourself.

September 15

Today's Self-Love Message:

Know that you are here for a purpose. Believe that you are evolving and working towards what you are meant to be. Everything is going as planned, even if you can't see it just yet. Continue to light the flame that is in your heart and share it. Let go of any worry at the end of each day and treat yourself to love.

Be the place where your body can rest easy.

September 16

Today's Self-Love Message:

Take care of yourself in every possible way. Trust that the universe will provide space for self-care as long as you create the intention to be present for your day-to-day needs.

Always love who you are in all that you do.

September 17

Today's Self-Love Message:

All you have to do is show up. Open your heart to receive the highest and truest good for your unfoldment. Believe in yourself and let that be the guiding force behind your personal connections. Join forces with your tribe and make magic happen!

There is a community for every one of us.

September 18

Today's Self-Love Message:

One day has got to be now. Create good feelings as much as possible. Laugh at the silly conversations you find yourself in. Recognize how quickly time goes by. This is your real life.

Be proud of who you are.

September 19

Today's Self-Love Message:

The body senses what you are going through on several levels. Tune in and listen to the messages you are receiving. Your heart is big enough to carry you through whatever life brings. You never know what could happen. Life is full of surprises!

You are a miracle.

September 20

Today's Self-Love Message:

It is okay to wait to ask for help until you know what you need. Just know that if you ever need anything, there is always someone here for you.

Ask when you are ready.

September 21

Today's Self-Love Message:

There is magic in the creation of life. Everything can change in an instant. You have the power to ask for what you want and can go make it happen! Know that the love of who you are is everlasting. Open your heart and embrace all that comes.

The light in you is bright.

September 22

Today's Self-Love Message:

The physical body grounds you to this reality. It allows you to feel and experience the world from your own unique perspective. Spend time in this body that makes up the person you are. Take care of yourself.

Go feel the earth!

September 23

Today's Self-Love Message:

You are embarking on a season of change. Shedding all of who you have been up until this time in your life. You are free to share your inner self without any barriers. The result of what you are going through is yours to decide.

Settle into yourself for this radical transformation.

September 24

Today's Self-Love Message:

Check in with your emotional wellness. Look for the small cracks that have caused pain in your life. Find out how you heal yourself by taking the time to mend your heart. Do what feels right and seek help if needed. Awareness of your thoughts and feelings gives you the space for self-discovery. You are full of positive energy, and that is what you came here to share with others and yourself.

Be in your own heart.

September 25

Today's Self-Love Message:

Start each morning with an intentional practice. Meditate for a few minutes and send golden healing light into your entire day. Self-love is taking the time to set your day up for success. Daily practices encourage the body to relax, feel safe, and align with higher-level frequencies. Go into your day knowing that positive energy has been sent forth in your life.

What can you do every day to make a major difference in your life?

September 26

Today's Self-Love Message:

You are always adding to your life. You go through experiences to learn what is right for you and what is not. Open your heart and allow the parts to fit together in perfect alignment.

You are always complete and always changing.

September 27

Today's Self-Love Message:

Fall in love with your life. Be so consumed with fulfilling your purpose that love is all you know. When you express who you are from a place of total acceptance, then other people are able to be who they need to be. You cause ripple effects in the world when you begin working on your own heart. Know that you are a work in process. You are always changing, shedding, and becoming who you are. Be proud of each accomplishment.

Greatness is yours.

September 28

Today's Self-Love Message:

Never give up on your vision and passion in life. The brighter you shine your light, the more exposed others will be to their own light.

Support is here for you.

September 29

Today's Self-Love Message:

Life starts and ends with you. You are the only person who will witness every part of your existence. Create a life you will flourish in. You cannot control all of the external forces, but you can be grateful in every situation. Be free of negative influences and know that as you work on yourself, you are changing the world. Your happiness is a part of the large collective.

Freedom is showing who you are to the world.

September 30

Today's Self-Love Message:

The time for transformation has arrived. It is in this moment that you will step over the threshold of where you have been. Accept what has brought you here and celebrate your journey. Release your fear of being on the wrong path. You are worthy of a prosperous and happy life!

Be alive in the life you have created.

October

October 1

Today's Self-Love Message:.

Float in the sea of allowing. You are always becoming the person you want to be.

Become all that you are destined to be.

October 2

Today's Self-Love Message:

Be fulfilled and grateful for all that has manifested for you. Open up to receive and keep growing from all that you are given.

Be proud of who you are.

October 3

Today's Self-Love Message:

Waiting is a skill that requires practice. You can't be too anxious for results or they get further from you. It is only coming to you if you are meant to have it. What can you do? You show up knowing that the promotions, houses, partners, and friends will arrive in the perfect time. Be grateful in the midst of waiting. Spend some time reflecting on all the wishes you have had come true. Give yourself credit for how far you have come.

You are one with all that is.

October 4

Today's Self-Love Message:

Take time every day for you. In this time, create a ritual to increase the bond you have with yourself. Promise yourself that you will do something that makes you feel whole and happy.

Practice daily self-love with intention.

October 5

Today's Self-Love Message:

Self-worth is a necessary component to manifesting your passions in life. You must fully believe you are worthy of receiving in order for the universe to deliver it to your doorstep.

You are worthy of your destiny.

October 6

Today's Self-Love Message:

You are here to expand your awareness and share your gifts with the world. When you reach your fullest capacity, you may settle momentarily, but then the next shift will begin. Eventually you will start all over again. It is about seeing each step in your life as an intricate necessary detail. You are here to rise up, do your part, and then get out of the way for the next process to begin. Even the most powerful beings on the planet will eventually just be soil. It gives an interesting perspective to how you view the people in your life. Put your roots down and grow to your highest potential.

Continue to stretch towards the sky.

October 7

Today's Self-Love Message:

Live with purpose by accepting that your identity changes as you experience more of life. Leaving behind the old can be so hard to do, especially if you don't want to let go. However hard it may seem, you must move in the direction of your path. You will not be taken down; you will only rise higher, more aware of another aspect of yourself. So often you stay or do things because you feel it is the right thing or to do. When your heart cries out to take a leap of faith, you must answer that call. Listen to it guide you and trust it to be the force that drives you.

Resolve to love yourself through it all!

October 8

Today's Self-Love Message:

Be in awe of who you are. There is not one person in this world who can be you.

What makes you special?

October 9

Today's Self-Love Message:

Knowing what you are called to do is the first step in bringing everything together to make it real. It is absolutely possible to live the life you want! Believe in yourself! Everything it takes to accomplish your goal is ready and waiting for you.

Ask and be ready to receive.

October 10

Today's Self-Love Message:

You are here to experience this life completely. Each time you share your love, make it bigger and better. Realize that it is what everything comes back to. Losing, finding, making, and forgetting, in all things, you are still love.

Let your heart be filled with loving gratitude.

October 11

Today's Self-Love Message:

Whatever you uncover in your quest to know and love yourself, you are capable of dealing with. Recognize that when you work on yourself, it can be a fragile time. Imagine that you have a fire burning inside of you and that you can put anything that no longer serves you into the flames. Burn away all that is holding you back.

Discover your glow.

October 12

Today's Self-Love Message:

Accepting the steady flow of change in your life will help you stay balanced. If you resist who you are, it is possible to create environments that can be depleting. You are not destined to stay in any one scene for your whole life. Do not fear the unknown. Trust you will look back and see the strength you possessed to leap without a net. You are here for a very specific purpose! Have faith that you will be supported in fulfilling all that you are meant to be in this lifetime.

It takes time to fulfill a life calling.

October 13

Today's Self-Love Message:

Love your life in all that you do. Let your love be the core of your experiences. When you experience life from your heart, it is so much more meaningful!

Choose to focus on the love in your life.

October 14

Today's Self-Love Message:

Open up to the beauty surrounding you. Connect with nature and feel the ground beneath you. This earth is your home. Let there always be peace in everything that you do.

There is power in every moment.

October 15

Today's Self-Love Message:

Live your truth and speak your mind. You have a gift to share. Be authentically you and let the world fall in love with all that you bring to the table.

What are you serving?

October 16

Today's Self-Love Message:

Every day when you wake up, there is so much wonder for what the day holds. Make a list of things you would like to accomplish and then set out to do just that. Let the day lead you to create exactly what you wanted.

Show up to your best life.

October 17

Today's Self-Love Message:

Listen to the wisdom speaking through your inner knowing self. Believe that if something feels wrong for you, then it absolutely is. When you trust yourself to know the answers of your heart, you can create the reality of your dreams. If you continue to stay when you know it is time to go, your life will surely suffer. Acceptance is the first step.

Which door opens to your destiny?

October 18

Today's Self-Love Message:

Connect with your tribe. Live for the moment and be yourself. Attract the conscious connections that you deserve. Be thankful to the people that you have meaningful relationships with. You are so fortunate to have one another.

What people are at the center of your circle?

October 19

Today's Self-Love Message:

Underneath all of the weight you are carrying is the brightest part of who you are. Remember no one sees who you are more than you. Take the time to nurture your soul with self-love and care. Grow to your fullest potential.

Drop what you no longer need to carry.

October 20

Today's Self-Love Message:

Light up from the inside and be proud of who you are. See the value you bring to the world. Recognize how important your life is and live in a way that brings renewal to your soul.

Trust what is happening.

October 21

Today's Self-Love Message:

Take care of yourself. Open up and receive the blessings that are all around you. Be with the people you love and let them fill your spirit. Let go of anyone who does not see you for the gift you are. If you are working on yourself, that's the best thing you can do. It's not up to anyone else how you live this life. Give to yourself what you want to be reflected in others. Accept help and opportunities knowing they are essential to your health. Be so in love with this gift of living that you are on a permanent vacation. What would it feel like to wake up and spend each day giving yourself the love you deserve?

All that is left to do is shine.

October 22

Today's Self-Love Message:

Take a day to be in your own element. Do whatever you want for an entire 24 hours! Drop into the spice of life and be filled with the love of everything that you are.

Let yourself have fun!

October 23

Today's Self-Love Message:

Sometimes the world feels out of balance and it can seem like you are giving more than you are receiving. This can be frustrating if you don't change your perspective. When you see other people getting what they want, that is a sign that you will also get whatever your heart is seeking. The more you witness other people making their way through life joyously, the closer you are to living the same way! Never give up!

You are worthy of living the life you deserve.

October 24

Today's Self-Love Message:

Release whatever is holding you back. This is not an easy job. You have to be willing to get dirty, work hard, and keep letting go as many times as you need to heal. Love this process, get to know what lifts the sadness from your heart, and take the time to figure it out.

You will always be able to see the way through.

October 25

Today's Self-Love Message:

Speak to your heart about how great you are and why you are thankful to be here today. Then turn that love out to the world so it can be shared and multiplied.

Lift yourself up.

October 26

Today's Self-Love Message:

Love your layers. Know your value in this life. You are equipped to handle any challenge you may face. Every experience adds a specific talent or skill to your original plan. Be open to having this human life bloom.

You are doing a great job!

October 27

Today's Self-Love Message:

Change is always here and you can benefit from it if you want to. It is possible to have left over remnants of your past still lingering around. Who you were several months ago is not the same person you are today. Ask yourself to release any blocks still left within you.

Life is a step-by-step process.

October 28

Today's Self-Love Message:

There are physical spaces on earth that feel more at home than others. Going there in your mind can be a way of connecting in with that specific energy. Memories are a way for you to be in another time or space. From the present moment, you can look back with understanding and compassion to see how far you have come. Persevere through whatever path you may climb.

Walk through the mountains of the mind.

October 29

Today's Self-Love Message:

The light is always in you. No matter what is happening, you are free to be the fullest expression of who you are. In everything you do, the best version of yourself shows up. There is never any need to try harder! You will make it to whatever you set your heart on.

Open your gate and let the light in.

October 30

Today's Self-Love Message:

This time could be the last time, so make it count. So often people in your life are taken for granted. It's not even on purpose. You just become accustomed to having them there. The same goes for other things like trees, oceans, rivers, and even your home. Be present, cherish the people you meet, love the scenery that is on a road to somewhere. Be in awe of all that you are and be thankful that you get another day.

Go into the world with gratitude.

October 31

Today's Self-Love Message:

You are being shown your path in everything you do. One way is through the guidance system in your body. Tune into how you feel in your current life experience. Trust that you will make choices that are in alignment with what is best for you.

There is no way except your pathway.

November

November 1

Today's Self-Love Message:

Who you are can shift constantly. This is not something you should fear. Learn about your perceptions and how they are impacting the world you live in. Be accountable for what you have created!

Your path is moving forward.

November 2

Today's Self-Love Message:

Gratitude begins with you. What you give out becomes the essence of who you are. If you want something to manifest, don't put all of your power into the future. Allow life to provide for you right now. See the magic of every moment. It's all about tuning into what feels right!

Be magical!

November 3

Today's Self-Love Message:

Make your own luck by believing in destiny. Know that you are able to create everything when you believe that you can.

All it takes is faith in the positive outcome.

November 4

Today's Self-Love Message:

Do your work and be proud of who you are right now. It took effort to create this life. Take credit for all that you are. Then do whatever it takes to keep moving forward. You deserve to be here and the world needs your energy.

Be joyful on your quest to accomplish your dreams.

November 5

Today's Self-Love Message:

Happiness is created by continually persevering to keep your thoughts positive. You are in control of how you react in every experience. By giving a bad situation or person attention, it amplifies and creates more of those negative situations in your life. The way to end the cycle is to acknowledge the experience, but change the focus. Step out of the pain by practicing non-attachment. Be aware of how much you are suffering due to your own inability to let things go. Next time you are feeling bad, allow the emotions to rise up. Acknowledge where they are coming from. Check in to see if it is something that belongs to you. Then take the necessary action. Believe you have the strength to bring your life back to a place of happiness.

This will change your life if you let it.

November 6

Today's Self-Love Message:

Dream of all your possibilities and know you are worthy. What perfect expression is within you? If everyone had inner peace and knew how to be loved, the world would change to a better place.

Be responsible for making peace. Begin within your own heart.

November 7

Today's Self-Love Message:

It is in the day-to-day actions that you build your life. One step at a time, no matter how advanced you become.

Light up your life.

November 8

Today's Self-Love Message:

When you wake up each day, give time to ease out of your dream state and into waking life. Slowly linger between the reality of your tasks ahead and the relief that comes from a good night's rest. Place your hands over your heart and visualize golden healing light coming to you and spreading out to the day ahead. How your day goes is not based on external forces, but rather how you decide to perceive them. Every day, fill your heart with love for this creation. It is from your own mind that the world manifests into reality.

Begin each day with a ritual.

November 9

Today's Self-Love Message:

Get the work done and then take time to be proud of what you have accomplished. Sometimes the best thing to do is persevere towards your goal. Other times it may be to step away and take a break. Notice that rest and action are essential to completing your goals. In balancing them, you are able to produce the most refined vision of your life.

Rest and action both require effort.

November 10

Today's Self-Love Message:

In every minute, you are evolving to the next. What a spectacular occurrence to have this current time and space in which you exist. Be your biggest observer. Care about what your intuition is telling you. Always remember you have endless opportunities.

You can always begin again.

November 11

Today's Self-Love Message:

Bring your attention to the roots in your life. Allow your mind to be filled with the remembrance of how it all happened. Suspend judgment on the memories and just observe how they are all a part of who you are. Life will link together circumstances and situations for your higher unfoldment. Review your life all the way to this present moment. Knowing where you came from is a part of who you are.

What is your foundation?

November 12

Today's Self-Love Message:

You are sitting on the edge of everything. Will you continue to stay on this ledge, or will you learn to trust your inner knowingness and take the leap? The time is always now. You have the answer. Let your passions come to life!

Your time has come.

November 13

Today's Self-Love Message:

It's always about working hard to get some rest. What if rest and taking a break was something you did just because you felt like it was needed? Stop making yourself do so much to be rewarded. Just always do your best and then stop when you need to. Give yourself a break and then extend that same action to those around you.

Be full of love for all that you are.

November 14

Today's Self-Love Message:

You have allowed whatever has come into your reality to be here. Your projection of life comes from your perception. What are you thinking about the most? What emotion dominates your day? Inquire within and notice how much of what you think about benefits your highest calling.

Infuse your existence with love.

November 15

Today's Self-Love Message:

It is better to run wild and free than sit around waiting to get to a solid destination. The journey of discovering where you belong can be filled with self-love and happiness! Look at the way a bridge holds up all the cars that pass over the water. It is capable of holding so much weight and never moves. It creates a pathway for others to travel on. What are you right now, the bridge holding everything up or the cars driving to a new destination?

Know when to stand strong and when to go with the flow.

November 16

Today's Self-Love Message:

Often, it is the choice everyone disagrees with that propels you to your next level. Go inside your mind, write down what you are thinking, and then analyze what it is. If it needs attention, then attend to your business. This is your biggest priority. You are already alive in perfection; you often just don't recognize it with ease. Discouragement, anger, and anxiety are indicators of deep-rooted unhappiness within. You must be able to address these wounds and heal them. Over time after you have healed, you will begin to uncover your new self. You will realize how it brought you to where you are right now. Acceptance is the sweetest gift you could ever give your heart.

Your happiness is worth it.

November 17

Today's Self-Love Message:

Love who you are, and you can do it all. It is that simple.

Accomplish your goals with ease.

November 18

Today's Self-Love Message:

Ask and have faith in receiving. You can build a new reality for yourself by recreating the way you think. Ask for whatever it is that your heart desires, and believe it is yours.

Be thankful for all that you have created.

November 19

Today's Self-Love Message:

Celebrate the life you have and expect the best in all that you do. Visualize yourself in alignment with the source of all things. Know that there is an eternal guiding light that is always with you. You are here for a little while, but you can make a difference that will last a lifetime.

Be legendary.

November 20

Today's Self-Love Message:

When the world feels like one rejection after the next and every effort was for someone else's gain, it is so hard to even muster up the words to comfort your soul. You turn to outside forces to find peace, rather than confront your own raging mind. It gets to the point where you are reminded that this has happened before in one way or another. How do you know what is at the bottom of all this pain? Ask your heart. The answers will lead to a story that will further your personal understanding. Eventually, as you listen to your thoughts and attend to your emotions, the body will naturally begin to calm down. It knows you are listening. It is similar to when you share what is on your mind with your friends. Express your feelings about what has come to the surface. Just talk it out with yourself and be present. Then understand that when the emotion arises again, you are uncovering another root. Repeat the process of self-inquiry each time. Work deeper and deeper until one day all you see is what is there after the pain has left.

You will make it!

November 21

Today's Self-Love Message:

Witness the depths of your humanness. When you explore who you are, then you are able to uncover deeper meaning about why you are here.

You have so many layers.

November 22

Today's Self-Love Message:

You have a purpose to fulfill. You are here because you are a survivor. No matter where you started, there is always a chance to remodel. It begins by paying attention to your thoughts and working with dedication on correcting negative beliefs about yourself and others.

Do what you love.

November 23

Today's Self-Love Message:

When you meet the love of your life, it is possible that you might pass them by. It will take time to find one another. Because meeting the other side of you will be monumental, causing such a shift that all that came before will seem insignificant to this new reality. In the meantime, before they get here, work on you. Spend the hours alone contemplating who you are. Love your darkness and make more room for your light.

Be thankful for the element of surprise.

November 24

Today's Self-Love Message:

Your body, mind, and spirit are capable of overcoming any obstacle.

Be alive in your soul.

November 25

Today's Self-Love Message:

There is always enough for you and plenty of time to experience it. Relax and enjoy all the pleasures right here. Be content with every passing day.

Hold space for your life.

November 26

Today's Self-Love Message:

Be kind to yourself. Know what that means to you. How does your day unfold when the first priority is caring about what you need to be successful? Whether you shine like glitter or feel like dirt, your reaction to the experience is how you shape the world around you.

React with a sense of security in whatever you experience.

November 27

Today's Self-Love Message:

You move through the storms of life to transform into something greater. If each trial were viewed as a breakthrough, it would feel less daunting. Peace means seeing chaos as a part of life. It is about not letting it become more than an observation. Clear your mind and take a deep breath. Ask to see yourself handling the situation peacefully. Paint a picture in your mind of a place that makes you feel calm and spend a few minutes getting to know this scene. Then apply the scene to the next chaotic moment. Witness what is happening and note that it is an external force. Maintain composure that you had prior to the experience. Then go to the peaceful place in your mind and regroup. The more often you practice conscious control of your thoughts, the more naturally they will spin in the direction that benefits your highest good.

You have the tools to put it altogether.

November 28

Today's Self-Love Message:

Open your heart to be loved. Experience the greatness of coming home to your own self. Know who and what you believe in. Say what is on your heart. Be honest with your emotions. Pour all of your energy into living your best life.

Make peace with whatever was before and move on to what is next.

November 29

Today's Self-Love Message:

You work every day to be the best version of yourself. When you give it your all, you expect the same from others. Whenever you look at someone else, always try to see the best in him or her. Here you are today, doing the best that you can and still improving all the time. Be proud of who you are! You are enough, and this life is your beautiful expression to the world.

Give yourself credit for the courage it takes to be you.

November 30

Today's Self-Love Message:

Even if all of your effort went into becoming what you are today, wanting something new is part of life. You are always working towards a goal, but when you get there, you may realize that a different path calls to you. Change is the only reliable thing in life, and it would benefit you to embrace it with open arms! What you are seeking is also looking for you.

Trust that your dreams want to come true.

December

December 1

Today's Self-Love Message:

Leave room to fill your cup. If you are afraid to use your favorite things because they will be gone, then you energetically express a lack in your ability to create more. Instead, use up what you have and love it! Then let it go and make space for more goodness to come in. This is something you need to do with all aspects of your life.

Make it your focus to have more space.

December 2

Today's Self-Love Message:

If you are always looking for the silver lining, you might miss what is in front of you. Smile more and laugh at the hard times. Be present wherever you are. This is what you should be doing! Always know that the silver lining is just the backdrop to your beautiful life.

This is your life.

December 3

Today's Self-Love Message:

You are the love that lights the way. Continue to serve your purpose to better yourself and the world around you. Create meaningful connections that open your heart. You are absolutely able to attract what you want into your life.

Shine your love for the world to see.

December 4

Today's Self-Love Message:

Let go and trust that everything is coming. There is no need to force anything. See your manifestations coming to fruition. When you open up to your life, you are able to experience all that is available to you.

Show up and be your greatest potential.

December 5

Today's Self-Love Message:

Negative thinking is similar to looking at the sky in all of its glorious color and labeling it as pollution. Positive thinking is acknowledging the truth and still admiring the splendor of what is. In every action or thought, we can decide where the attention goes. No matter how bad something seems, you can always decide to keep your peace.

What are you choosing to see in your reality?

December 6

Today's Self-Love Message:

When your safety is at risk, it is normal to question why. This happens so that you can learn how to remain stable even when you are faced with the trials of humanity. Stand proud in the face of adversity. Even though you are tempted to shut down, remain open. See yourself through to the completion of whatever you had to experience.

Life will be a safe place if you allow it to be.

December 7

Today's Self-Love Message:

When life is a struggle and everything seems overwhelming, it is very easy to forget self-love. Sadness and loss are a part of being human. The best thing to do when faced with trauma is to sit down, close your eyes, and check in with your heart. Ask yourself what is the matter? Listen for the answers. Let the waves of emotions roll through. Once you have uncovered the dilemma, create a space to facilitate healing. Being here, for your own heart, is the greatest act of love in the world.

Love changes everything around you.

December 8

Today's Self-Love Message:

Experience the fullness of life! Tune into love in all that you do.

Keep creating a better experience.

December 9

Today's Self-Love Message:

Pause and admire all that has happened before now. Then be present for just a moment. Can you see how everything always worked out? Most of the time it was when you exerted the least amount of effort that the biggest growth occurred. Even though you are often given signs of overworking, you continue to push through, exhaust all effort, and drain the life from your heart. Take the time to relax and receive the gift of being alive.

Enjoy who you are now.

December 10

Today's Self-Love Message:

Contentment is time spent enjoying life. Sit and appreciate your surroundings. Listen to your heart and give love to yourself every day. What brings inner peace? Make it a daily task to cultivate more joy in your life.

Be conscious of your actions.

December 11

Today's Self-Love Message:

Throughout this year, many circumstances have brought you closer to yourself. Knowing how to love yourself has taught you how to accept love from others. It is a free love. No matter who comes or goes, the person who you are is what matters.

Loving yourself brings a new meaning to being loved by others.

December 12

Today's Self-Love Message:

You might wonder how your perception impacts others. When you exude peace, you bring that to the world. What vibe are you paying attention to? If you often feel bad, that is a guidepost to say that your focus is on the negative. You are important and how you feel matters. Listen to your heart, focus your mind on positive thinking, and live the life you deserve.

Even the most insignificant times of life hold meaning.

December 13

Today's Self-Love Message:

Love is always perfect timing. All you have to do is work on loving who you are. When you have an unshakeable foundation of self-love, you open the door to allow others to love you. Not in any random way, but exactly how you want to be loved.

Be loved.

December 14

Today's Self-Love Message:

Trust in who you are becoming. You are constantly changing and evolving into yourself. Allow the gifts of wisdom to keep moving you forward. It just keeps getting better every day. Let this be your mantra for life! Believe in the possibility of your ever-expanding greatness.

You've got this!

December 15

Today's Self-Love Message:

Spend time in nature to reconnect with your soul. Reestablish your connection to Mother Earth. The more time you spend in communion with nature, the better you are able to handle what comes to you. The answers you seek are waiting for you in the stillness of the natural world.

Go outside and find your peace.

December 16

Today's Self-Love Message:

The act of holding anger or ill will in your heart permeates your current reality. It is absolutely impacting every aspect of your life. Forgiveness is freedom from pain and suffering. You have the power to transmute negative energy into something more beneficial for you. When you feel a strong negative emotion towards a person or experience, that is an indication that you need to forgive. Acknowledge the emotions and see if you can uncover what is causing it. Whether or not an exact memory comes up, set the intention to be released from the bonds of heartache. Wrap the situation in loving kindness and let it go. If it helps to imagine handing it to a higher power, then do it!

Forgive and heal.

December 17

Today's Self-Love Message:

Release the weight of the world on your shoulders. Renew your spirit by spending at least a few minutes every day in quiet meditation. This is incredibly healthy for your soul.

Spend time in quiet reflection every day.

December 18

Today's Self-Love Message:

Receiving guidance is helpful. Another person's point of view can allow you to see your own life from a different perspective.

Magic is alive in you.

December 19

Today's Self-Love Message:

Decide on a new path never traveled before. Prepare your gear so that you will have the comforts of any need that must be met. Spend the resources necessary to make sure all is well. Life is waiting for your next big move! What will it be?

Adventure makes your heart grow.

December 20

Today's Self-Love Message:

Release anything that is less than what you want to experience in your life.

Focus on forward movement!

December 21

Today's Self-Love Message:

What would happen if you slowed down enough to actually acknowledge the passing of time? You would notice the intricate details that make up the world around you. You would have solid proof that rushing gets you nowhere fast. It's about holding on to the precious gift of life for as long as you can.

Stop rushing.

December 22

Today's Self-Love Message:

Every day should feel good, and gratitude is the best way to make it happen.

You are perfect and wonderful.

December 23

Today's Self-Love Message:

Open up to a deeper understanding of how life works by completely surrendering. Reach for greater potential by accepting all that is happening right now.

Release and let the light in.

December 24

Today's Self-Love Message:

Write down your thoughts because the way in which you perceive your life is what you are creating outside of yourself. Bring forth your purpose with diligent persistence and remove what does not serve your best interests. Let the brilliant ideas that have been just outside of your awareness flood in!

You are so essential to this place.

December 25

Today's Self-Love Message:

Loving who you are is such a gift to give to the whole world. When you create your own happiness, you make this place a happier one to coexist in. Imagine if everyone on Earth loved and accepted who they are! When you are one with body and mind, anything is possible. It always comes back to loving who you are.

Cherish the moments you want to last forever.

December 26

Today's Self-Love Message:

In each of you is the answer to peace. You are the creator of your own happiness. You bring joy to the world. Add more stillness to your life by appreciating the in-between moments. These are the sweet spots in life--quiet reflections within your soul that lead to your expansion.

To know the heart is to love the mind.

December 27

Today's Self-Love Message:

The more consciously you exist, the easier you are able to transition from one moment to the next. Allow space between thought and action to give way to better and better choices. Your self-love presents itself to those you come in contact with. Let the energy spill over to those you meet. Know how connected you are.

Be the change you need.

December 28

Today's Self-Love Message:

Love to be with yourself. Quiet days filled with stillness and purpose makes forward progress even more accessible. Celebrate life for all that it is. See your downtime as important to your overall health. Everything will work out the way it should.

You have so much to offer yourself.

December 29

Today's Self-Love Message:

What a feeling it is to be surprised by the universe and timing. Everything can change in a chance meeting that leads to so many different possibilities. Acknowledge when it happens and celebrate the good news. It is supposed to work out for you! You are meant to experience joy and true love. Let it all come to you.

The possibility is always there.

December 30

Today's Self-Love Message:

Close your eyes and imagine what your dream reality looks like. You are not here to suffer or want for unattainable goals. You are here to receive what your heart's desires. Once this really makes sense, everything will change. You grow stronger all the time, and it is because you keep going. It is worth it, and there is so much to love about who you are.

Make the world better by loving yourself.

December 31

Today's Self-Love Message:

Love your life and be happy to be here. You are capable and will accomplish anything you desire. You have all the answers. Listen to your inner guidance. Every day is a new opportunity to be in love with who you are.

Love is all that matters.

Afterword

Each of these passages was written daily
over the entire year of 2017.

Afterword

CPSIA information can be obtained
at www.ICGtesting.com
Printed in the USA
LVHW09s1306100918
589682LV00001B/9/P